THE FARTING CHRISTMAS

COLORING BOOK

M.T. LOTT

**Share your colored pages
on instagram @mtlottbooks**
#christmasfarts

Sign up for free coloring pages at
www.MTLottBooks.com

Connect with M.T. Lott on facebook
www.facebook.com/authormtlott

BOOKS BY M.T. LOTT

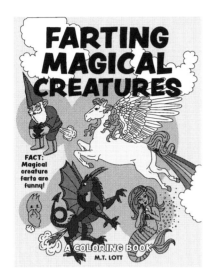

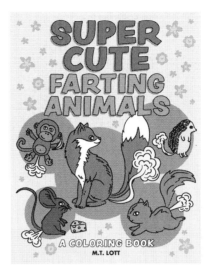

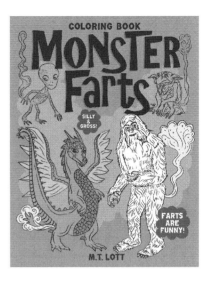

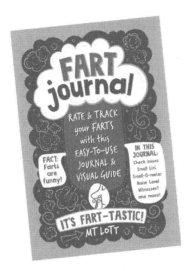

Available for purchase at your favorite on-line bookstore.

Join my email list and get FREE coloring pages
www.MTLottBooks.com

Do you know the real reason why Santa touches the side of his nose?

Colored by:

Date:

Beware the Christmas pug
air biscuit.

Colored by:

Date:

Birds are careful of the
Snowman's wintry blast.

Colored by:

- -

Date:

Squirrels give each other
extra presents.

Colored by:

Date:

Run, run as fast as you can...
away from Gingerbread Man farts.

Colored by:

Date:

We all know who cuts
the Christmas cheese.

Colored by:

Date:

It's pretty awful when there's a fart trapped in the snowglobe.

Colored by:

Date:

The sugar plum fairy dance
is gracefully flatulent.

Colored by:

Date:

Reindeer farts sound
like jingle bells.

Colored by:

Date:

Mrs. Claus has to be careful
how many cookies she eats.

Colored by:

Date:

Colored by:

Date:

Thank goodness it's a
one horse *open* sleigh!

Colored by:

Date:

Find the wonder of Christmas farts in all of nature's creatures.

Colored by:

Date:

The farting Cardinal is the first
sign of the season.

Colored by:

Date:

Christmas bear wants to
give you a present.

Colored by:

Date:

The nutcracker sometimes shocks himself.

Colored by:

Date:

Penguins like to cut loose at the
annual ugly sweater party.

Colored by:

Date:

Elves leave a little something
extra behind.

Colored by:

Date:

Fact: You can fart in a snowsuit to keep warm.

Colored by:

Date:

On the first day of Christmas
my true love sent to me...
a gassy partridge.

Colored by:

Date:

Colored by:

Date:

Some elf games are gross.

Colored by:

Date:

Do you know the real reason why
Santa touches the side of his nose?

Colored by:

- -

Date:

Beware the Christmas pug
air biscuit.

Colored by:

Date:

Birds are careful of the
Snowman's wintry blast.

Colored by:

Date:

Squirrels give each other extra presents.

Colored by:

Date:

Run, run as fast as you can...
away from Gingerbread Man farts.

Colored by:

Date:

We all know who cuts
the Christmas cheese.

Colored by:

Date:

It's pretty awful when there's a fart trapped in the snowglobe.

Colored by:

Date:

The sugar plum fairy dance
is gracefully flatulent.

Colored by:

Date:

Reindeer farts sound
like jingle bells.

Colored by:

Date:

Mrs. Claus has to be careful
how many cookies she eats.

Colored by:

Date:

Colored by:

Date:

Thank goodness it's a
one horse *open* sleigh!

Colored by:

Date:

Find the wonder of Christmas farts
in all of nature's creatures.

Colored by:

Date:

The farting Cardinal is the first sign of the season.

Colored by:

Date:

Christmas bear wants to give you a present.

Colored by:

Date:

The nutcracker sometimes
shocks himself.

Colored by:

Date:

Penguins like to cut loose at the
annual ugly sweater party.

Colored by:

Date:

Elves leave a little something
extra behind.

Colored by:

Date:

Fact: You can fart in a snowsuit to keep warm.

Colored by:

Date:

On the first day of Christmas
my true love sent to me...
a gassy partridge.

Colored by:

Date:

Colored by:

Date:

Some elf games are gross.

Colored by:

Date:

Made in the USA
Coppell, TX
21 December 2019